CEPHALOPRESS
www.cephalopress.com

i

Published in the UK by Cephalopress Ltd 2021

Lannie Stabile

**Good Morning to Everyone Except Men
Who Name Their Dogs Zeus**

www.cephalopress.com

info@cephalopress.com

ISBN   978-1-8382206-1-7

Cover and book design by: Daniel Lambert

Lannie Stabile

Good Morning to Everyone Except Men Who Name Their Dogs Zeus

Cephalopress Ltd

Content warning:
This collection explores themes that readers may find distressing. Some poems contain descriptions of sexual assault, rape, flashbacks, dealing with trauma, and depression.

GOOD MORNING
TO EVERYONE
EXCEPT MEN
WHO NAME
THEIR DOGS
ZEUS

Contents

For the survivors.

Consent is not a myth.

Image by Koss

Lighting strikes in 5 ways:

Lannie Stabile

Leda

If you've ever seen swans fuck,
you'd know

it's a folded napkin in a dither,
while a second lays flat, soiled,
praying for dinner to end.

The male tops the female
in a freshwater body.

She must float them both.
She is submerged, beak beneath
the ripples, lost to the jaw
around her noose-length neck.

The deed lasts eight seconds.
After, he glides to the edge of the
pond, distancing himself from her,
while she honks, reaching back,
trying also to rid herself of him.

Zeus appeared to Leda
as a swan, then raped her.

Lannie Stabile

For the Birds

The wingspan of a mistake
is wide
Like a mockingbird diving
mouth-first

Like a dead duck

Lannie Stabile

1.Side Flash

Lighting is a stranger
in a bar, propped up
at the end of a pool table,
his eyes on you,
his hands on his zipper,
returning, even after the bouncer
says, *hey man,*
take that shit outside

I Can't Talk About It

My gut, that vengeful city of insomniacs,
swaps tales of trauma with the loose twilight.

Terrified of optimistic things, like the sun, it
drowns my sealed lips in caffeine. I survive

on muddy irrigation and anxiety, hollowed and
hungry, nibbling on fingertips that stretch

for perfect words, and refuse to let anyone
within spitting distance of this soft underbelly.

My tongue, that talented freight train, has been
known to tap out the rhythm to *Anything Goes*,

but when anything went, everything went, and I
am going anywhere and everywhere. Are you

following? I can't talk about it. It's like a scream
that keeps getting caught in my throat, but the

scream is a pair of men's hands, and his
cufflinks snag my vocal cords. Just like his

fingers snagged my closed eyes, dragging
me from a peace I will never have again. My

mouth, that deceitful poet, spoke forgiveness,
but how can I forgive my skin collapsing in on

itself? My bones drop away, even as I stand here,
and the only thing I can do to stay together is

shove myself into pockets of an oversized sense
of loss because I swallowed his apology and

his three paintings of a single taupe flower. As
if jeering at the femininity he stripped from me.

As if he knew this was the fifth time my body
has been deadened in this way. My womanhood,

that lost and weakened wheel squeaks, even
as I weep to keep things moving along. Every

day I am misrepresenting myself: Am I the
apple, the serpent, or the whole damn rib cage?

Protecting a man who refused to protect me. For
years, I have been howling on the inside, raking

my soul red and raw with the need to tear this story
out of my body, and still I can't talk about it.

Callisto

Arrogant king	Zeus
noticed a woman	was
tracking the hot stars	
of a goddess sky,	
and he translated	
Callisto into a	prideful
challenge	
With	in
huntress Artemis skin	
he took servant	Callisto's
modesty and pulled	
from her belly	
a new moon	conversion
Artemis, seeing	
what Daddy had ruined,	
made Callisto a bear	from maiden
then ran	
a bolt through her chest	
Yet, the goddess	
still loved her	
little bear	
and Callisto became	
a constellation	to flicker

The Effects of Lightning on the Human Body

Found poem with the substitution of "lightning" for "rape"

Like a gunshot, it causes
            both exit & entrance wound,

                              marking the victim.
                  White-hot substances

            burn. Clothing shredded,
    shoes & socks thrown off.

                  Many survivors do not
                      remember being struck.

The only evidence is burnt,
            displaced clothing

                      & marks along the body.
                  It will cook brain cells,

rendering them useless.
Memory issues.

Trouble with concentration.
Severe headaches.

All of which last decades
after the initial strike.

*Adapted from "The Effects of a Lightning Strike on the Human Body" by Kiri Picone, from allthatsinteresting.com

Depression Wakes Me Up
in the Morning

Today
I will not survive
with my knees
between my teeth

and the cold, jeering tile
Its hands searching
for the warmest parts
My horoscope warns
it is risky to slink into a body
with its back to you

today
I will not survive
with my knees

unprepared for grief
Feet still toasty
from the pocket of escape
I am a fatigued tempest
pinned in the cotton,
and I think I'll stay here

today
I will not survive

the shower
the car
the brunch he is attending
the social, predatory
pillory of

today

Zeus Was Called Daddy

Russian peasant Feodor Vassilyev sired 87
children / He holds the record for his litter //
Zeus was called Daddy by Greek gods and
worshippers alike / He fathered roughly 100
pups / making Feodor look like a whelping bitch
// The difference is while Feodor lay with two
women / Zeus screwed:

Themis	Thalia	Thalassa
Selene	Persephone	Nemesis
Mnemosyne	Metis	Maia
Leto	Hera	Gaia
Eurydome	Eris	Eos
Avanke	Aphrodite	Aega

And those were just the deities

Europa

I

She was a quarter-gone girl,
fresh of farm, with suede hands,
herding in each sun with her father.
Zeus, horny in a white bull cloak,
approached her half-gone pasture.
Taken by the animal,
with pretense mild as a cow,
she caressed his velvet flanks.
With the day three-quarters gone,
the gingerbread girl grew tired.
In search of rest,
she mounted the deceptive god,
and his jaws unhinged to guzzle her
all gone.

II

Some say Europa called the beast
to her river.
But there was never more bullshit
than a tale of a man
washing himself clean.

A God Is Not a Good Man

Though our mothers teach us
how to press our rage against fists
—the great muffler of grief—
sometimes a man kneads his way
into soft palms
and is stunned to find callousness there

He takes a virgin and mutates her
into a parable:
How if a woman cannot sense the beast
in the gentle animal,
the beast will burrow himself
into the gentlewoman

A man may be tempted to lie
in the grass, ready to swagger
Ready to strike
He will do this to prove his godliness,
the reaving of an innocent
Rather than leave her
working in the fields, untouched.

2.Ground Current

Lightning is an afternoon nap
with a cousin, waking
to curious hands
yawning along your stomach,
wondering how long
you've been asleep.

My Mother Deftly Misses the Point

I tell her, *Billy stares at me.*
Billy of the ponytail, of the chatter,
of the unpaid rent.
Billy, the virtual stranger,
whom I beg my mother
not to invite to Thanksgiving.

He may have a lazy eye,
she theorizes.

Billy of the eyes I know are blue
and alert
because of how often I find them
across the room
and on my ass.

I tell her I won't come to dinner
if Billy is there.

She ignores the ultimatum and asks,
Are you sure you don't mean Tim?

His Worst-Case Scenario

Her smile is the third curve
that tattoos his eye.
He licks at the plump zero
her lips carve out, when
surprised by his wolf whistle.
Her insecurity is sirenic.
He invites her to dinner.

It may scrape his mind
whether or not she's *the one*.
She isn't.
She has Instagram and
an associate degree.

She lets him kiss her once,
but treads midnight alone.
He is horny, disappointed.
The night was a total bust,
the company was lackluster,
the meal mediocre.
He wants his fifty bucks back.

Alcmene

sometimes	a predator
must	borrow
the	hus-
band's	face
to seduce	the wife

Husk

Husk is a strange word to climb into

I would rather *woman*
I would rather *whole*
Even *gunslinger* would do

I am of sheet, I am specter
I am expecting the lights and din to swallow me

Because they did once
—his palms stoic deserts, tumbleweeds rolling
along my ghost town body—
and all I remember is

the number of blades on the ceiling fan is five

God Help Us, Another Douchebag Has Named His Dog Zeus

a puppy nips
at his owner's fingers

and is not reprimanded
because

dogs will be
dogs

the gangly puppy
too large paws

soon will fuck
the neighborhood bitches

he can smell the heat
between their legs

and does not yet care
to master his senses

and the puppy swells
into full-grown mutt

who rejects commands
like wait and no

but will roll over
an unconscious body

behind a dumpster
and *come*

Fettered

Pulling his chain from between my legs,
links groaning along thighs
slick with struggle,

he drained me

In This Olympian House, We

🖊 suckle at the teat of a nanny goat, nourishing our
lucent bodies until we are swole and tyrannical

🖊 are both the youngest and eldest siblings; crowing
grandfathers and bawling children

🖊 wield lightning bolts like we're in the throes of
puberty, and the bathroom door is locked

🖊 disguise ourselves as animals, fuck every woman
we see, licking at dalliance or entanglement or
conquest but never rape

🖊 swallow our first wives to avoid patricide, but our
daughters still spring forth from her father's skull

🖊 marry our sisters, call them snacks

🖊 punish a thief, whose crime was keeping his family
warm, by chaining him to a rock and siccing
eagles on his liver

🖊 gulp our children down like eggs, one by one, until
there is no one left to challenge the skies, the seas,
and the pits of inevitable hell

↗ appear to our lovers — naked and glorious — only to destroy her in an instant, and bind her into the thick meat of our bodies

↗ precipitate into golden showers

↗ rape a priestess to humiliate a god, then curse her, as a treat

↗ unleash a great flood upon the earth with the sole purpose to wipe out mankind — unscrupulous and wretched

When My Therapist Asks Me to Explain What 90 Seconds of Safety Feels Like, I Can Only Think of One Example

When she asks if I need anything,
I want to say *milk* or *water* or *nothing*
Something easy to swallow
Unlike this stump,
which has shed so many useless branches,
my throat can no longer grow around the bark

The first time I creak *lemon ginger tea*
through my tight, nervous pulp,
I wait for the *no* to seep in
But she boils the water, steeps the bag, and hands off
the steaming mug like it's a sleeping child

And I cannot reconcile this with the request
I have seen splintered
into a century's worth of deep cut
rings of disappointment and betrayal and humility

The tea, if it was ever present in my folktales
before, was only an instrument for
drowning

How Many Hands
Does the Trout Have?

The last river that touched me
shot down the mountain
like a bullet through a ruddy duck.
Impatient and entitled,
water spilled into my mouth
before a wave could swell.
And, try as I might,
I could not avoid the jumping fish.
In my arms, in my lap, between lips
too tired to dam the currents.

"Barnabas, They Called Zeus"
(Acts 14:12)

If Zeus is named in the Bible,
does that make him a brown god

                turned white or a bleached swan
                turned gilded bull? With paws in

maidens up to the cufflinks, saint
is a thick word stretched thin on

                nymph tongues. And out of sex and
                cumulus clouds, Zeus made apostles.

3.Conduction

Lightning is two hands
cradling hips,
while Kaci Battaglia
and Ludacris lick
through club speakers,
an erection nudging
the small of your back.

Lannie Stabile

The Plural of Cyclops is Cyclopes

A girl can carry her drink to the bathroom,
or a friend can guard it within her wool.

She can spot and uproot red flags
like a row of Washington Apples.

A girl can call an Uber,
or substitute water for undiluted wine.

A girl can travel in a flock,
or tuck keys between her knuckles

like Hellenistic soldiers.
She can even master Krav Maga

and the myth of prevention.
A girl can occupy a barstool all night long,

with a vigilant eye on her glass,
but when the SAFE kit is processed

in the morning, police will insist
there is nobody to blame.

Lannie Stabile

Medusa Haiku
Five for Medusa, A Priestess Not Raped by Zeus, but Bro Poseidon

Beauty is a stone
cast by men wielding tridents
in tight, hungry fists

She was no monster
But a woman in temple,
sacrificed to gods

Even when she said,
I am still worthy, she was
decapitated

Athena may have
cast the curse, but Poseidon
is the fucking snake

Lannie Stabile

Her Worst-Case Scenario

He grins, *hello*
Lips, nose, and eyes
are a handsome constellation
He makes her laugh
Shows just enough interest
to keep her guessing
Then suggests dinner

He tells her about his non-profit,
his dreams, and his tabby
And thoughtfully probes her
for more profound stats
They share a kiss and a cab

His hands are shards
when he rapes and kills her
Shredding wrists and thighs
Tearing them wide open
His lips, nose, and eyes
are a black hole
as he makes her disappear

When I Tell Friends My Therapist Suggested Anger Management, They All Say, *But You Don't Get Angry*

My therapist hands me a padded club
and points to a couch
pressed against the wall
Hit it. Go on.
And I stand there,
with the answer blistering in my fist

But beating the shit out of a lumpy sofa
indicates a loss of self-control
and command of my own body

My therapist asks me
to put my hands to his shoulders and push
him away, screaming, *No*
Over and over again until my objection
bounces around the room

Even as I strike the bone
of his button-up shirt,
I refuse to burst

My therapist tells me to plant my feet
firmly on the ground,

breathe deeply,
and say, *I am good enough*

The lie clings to my mouth
like a hot palm

How to Define Depression

I am a noun. The last three movies I've watched depict nature and sexual violence, and I haven't figured out yet that I'm triggered as a motherfucker. Been trying to speak for hours, but my lips are fish fading in the dirt. My wife holds my head in her lap, and snot rivers from one nostril to the thigh of her blue jeans, as I hiccup hiccup hiccup. It is proof of my vulnerability. *It's all right, it's all right,* she coos, but I am still afraid of appearing messy.

I am an adjective, too. There is something broken. A moment ago, I was laughing. Now, I am a berry bush, trying my best not to be poisonous. I think, *I am not good enough.* And the sentence wraps my body like a ring toss. Again and again, until I cannot tell the age of the rot.

Sometimes, I am even a verb. I splash water on my face, like a self-baptizing flower, and wipe the weakness away. I can't help but consider it all a waste of time — intimacy and the exorcism of pain — when I could have been doing more productive things. Like ridding myself of infected trees. Like deforestation. Like spray-painting a bright red X on my bark.

Metis

Before Hera, there was Metis
Before 7th wife, there was 1st

Before goddess of women,
there was goddess of counsel

Before a god who loved women,
there was a god who would take no counsel

Because his mouth buzzed for Hera's form,
Zeus tricked Metis into becoming a fly,
then promptly swallowed her

Throughout history, men have bungled breakups

4.Streamers

Lightning is slamming
your 7-year-old body
against a 6-foot Joe Dumars
poster, and an older boy,
with virile insistence,
stealing your first kiss.

Lost Child

innocence / runs away
with nothing
but a stick and a sack

a blade / of grass grows taller
than the lost child

mistakes are made / by the innocent
way she marks him
as holy

it is the childhood / she loses

These Boots Are Made for Trauma

My feet
are wearied and jaded
As a pair,
one incites the other
like Thelma pleading to Louise,
Let's keep going

And there is a certain
suicide
to the rhythm
of rubber slapping
the cheeks of a street on which
a boy
first wore me out

But *let's keep going*
Keep pushing toes into
a too-tight boot,
flesh rubbing against death
This life
is bound to eventually fit

Lannie Stabile

Menagerie of Deception

Encyclopaedia Britannica Erasure

Zeus, in ancient sky,
was nursed by
                warrior
manhood.
The logical home for a weather god is
                atop
a dispensing daughter.
Zeus was a source of love
affairs
with animals:
                a cuckoo
                a swan
                a bull
                a bearded eagle.

I Wish I Had the Foresight of Charlene Wood

I'd like to think I have regular, meaningful conversations with my body. Less good *morning* and *good night*, and more *how are you, really* and *you make me proud*. I'd like to think we are close enough and in-sync enough, that goosebumps are rumble strips, a crabwise gut is a trigger, and a tremoring bridge is *let's get the fuck out of here*. I'd like to think, based on a shaky hunch, I'd reverse my '67 Pontiac to solid land, mouthing a horrified prayer for the car ahead. Instead of sliding along with it into the dark depths of the Ohio River. I'd like to think I wouldn't have been the 47th person to perish on Silver Bridge.

But I don't trust myself

Sometimes, even when I know I'm full, I keep eating. Sometimes, when office gossip is #metoo and sexy celebrity rapists, I pretend I'm not a compilation of flashbacks. Sometimes, when the fist is flying, I don't dodge it.

Lannie Stabile

Michigan Tech University, Winter Festival, 2006
After tweet by @spinubzilla

My favorite trope is
when shy girl is
uncharacteristically chugging beer
at 8am frat party
but attends school 500 miles away,
so has no one
but best friend to answer to.
When she's virgin
but hat tricking
with nerdiest bros,
including moppy-headed Joe,
who sleeps in Chapter house closet.
When she Quiz Bowls
but also keg stands.
When she is historically cautious
but presently wasted.
When she grew up ponytail,
glasses, low self-esteem
but also has boobs
against two hot girls in kitchen,
boys pulling out phones
and cocks,
making the best of the moment.

Ganymede

When a beautiful boy walks by,
    Zeus is equal opportunity predator,
and his head snaps back like a meme
    When a beautiful boy walks by,
electricity thrums in the god's groin
    He becomes horny eagle
and talons boy up the mountain
    When a beautiful boy walks by,
the boy is sold as a vivid moon
    placed in the darkest side of heaven
When a beautiful boy walks by,
    Zeus substitutes horses for dowry,
tells his father-in-law, with a wink,
    I'll have him home by 10, Daddy

Slasher Flicks Are Often Parables on Life-Long Healing

I'm sitting on the couch
watching a horror movie

and eating Pad Thai
with crushed peanuts,

even though I am allergic.
So what if my throat shrinks

when the one thing
I really need to talk about

is a decade old event
that gets bigger every day.

Words tumble in my mouth,
clunky and expired

like bodies in an industrial dryer.
A memory looping, looping.

I think about Brandy
in I Still Know

What You Did Last Summer,
how her scream fell out

with the dead laundress,
but snagged

at Mekhi's spontaneous
tracheotomy.

Like Miss Norwood,
I've developed calluses

on my fingers from counting
how many times I've relived

a drunken summer party.
How many times I had too many

wine coolers washed down
with agave-flavored peer pressure.

My throat closes up
when I remember how

I walked into that room voluntarily,
his tongue the only hook in my lip.

Our clothes the only dirty
linen tumbling.

Dreadlocked Jack Black
was stoned when he died,

garden shears
piercing his Hawaiian shirt.

I too have been impaled
while intoxicated.

And I can tell you
senses are not dulled,

but alive and kicking
the sheets off the bed.

Sometimes your friend
is the man in the slicker,

holding an ice hook
to your trembling body,

daring you to move
on from the previous summer.

As I spoon rice noodles
into a mouth

open only for danger,
I taste the sweet nuttiness

of unmitigated risk
and watch the credits roll.

5.Direct Strike

Lightning is a friend
offering solace
with a tongue
between your legs,
and when he repositions himself,
you say, I'*m not really sure* —
and he says, *too late*

When Depression Talks Over Me

When I said I was beginning to heal,
I meant pieces of my past have been breaking off
in painful, messy ways
And I thought the cobbles and pebbles
would bind together to form neat steppingstones,
so I would know where the hell I'm going
But they've washed away in a flood of self-deprecation

I am honestly rubble at this point
A body pile that was once shelter,
was once woman
With a doorbell and hands
and impostor syndrome
Don't waste your time rifling through this chaos
If you're looking for a way in,
please know the door did not survive the storm

When I said I could breathe again,
I meant my body has unwedged itself
from beneath a boulder
It is damaged and flatter than any tone I can dredge up
when I tell you, I'm just taking it day by day

I am salt and flour and sugar
I am built from three levels
of a special kind of perdition,
rolled into my own stubborn boulder

with a self-centered center
Then stretched from one end of the earth to the other,
my skin thinning every time I realize
I'm not a perfect anything
Until you can finally see through me

When I said I recently learned how to cry,
I meant my emotions tried to drown me
in my own fucking sea
I was not born a social animal,
and I've never learned to talk to boats or fish or sirens
Anything that might carry me to the shore
So, here I am, choking on a petty memory,
as the tide rushes down my throat

I remember the first time I unhinged my jaw,
vomiting the swollen stories,
watching them gurgle in the open air
I wanted to swallow them down again, like eggs,
whole and white and weak
I thought if I was lucky, maybe they would lodge there,
in that perfect space between mind and gut
And I would finally have a physical reason to collapse

When I said I was starting to feel like myself again,
I meant in the night, I met a monster
who looked so much like me
that when she offered rest, it felt natural
for her to slip into these dark, weary veins

When Depression Talks Over Me

I licked a shattered mirror once,
searching for the flavor of pieces
that could no longer recognize
their misanthropic edges
She, rather I, tasted like teeth and knees
I've tried washing my mouth out
with carbonated therapy,
but her, rather my, desperation lingers

When I said the future looked brighter,
I meant I've been combusting all along,
hurling toward an angry star

Danaë

Imagine a man
so insecure
he precipitated
his body
into piss itself
to impress a woman

To impress upon her
how potent he was

To press into her

Damp and lustful, Zeus
slipped through a skylight,
into a locked chamber,
and within her lap

Maybe this worked
less like magic
and more like science
Like evaporation
Except instead of rising
into a cloud,
it was Danaë

And that rain bore a son
who would stone a woman
whose only sin was being
infiltrated by a man

Lannie Stabile

Letter to a Rapist

July 4, 2007

Dear Z-,

You are the long, slender neck of a swan, contorting at angles that could stuff a body in a suitcase. A fly in the jaws of a thunderstruck god. A shriek through the sacred mountains of an upper middle-class home.

You are a king and a tyrant, quiet hand creeping beneath the covers at a sleepover. Eagle tapping at the window, begging to enter, to carry childhood away.

You are a rowdy midsummer festival. Nectar served in solo cups, the smooth, red sides echoing maiden blood. A pool. A hot tub. A looming throne. Sky blue wallpaper retreating from the mattress, a casualty shrinking to the size you have made her feel.

You are the armored migraine, springing forth fully nightmare. A monster beneath the belly of a bed.

You are a flash flood drowning calves in the field. A storm unseen in the clouds. The kind of lightning that keeps a girl awake for twenty years, wondering what it is about her body that calls to all the winds.

-L

Lannie Stabile

Acknowledgements

To start, I want to thank my mother, who was gone before she could hold this book in her hands. Thank you for teaching me to take chances. I don't know where I'd be in life without that lesson. Thank you to my wife, Kaitlyn, who gives me the space and encouragement to write and submit, even when I'm spending all our money on submission fees. Thank you to Maté Jarai and Amy Smith for putting so much thought, effort, and belief into editing this collection. Thank you to Jason B. Crawford who continuously pushes me and always brings snacks to our writing sessions. Thank you to Eric Sirota for sitting next to me and Jason that day; your friendship is like a Jewish space laser. Thank you to Maddie Corley, who has indefatigably read every angry Zeus poem I've ever written. Thank you to Jason Ramsey for unwavering support and confidence in abilities I never knew I had. Thank you to the friends I've met on Lit Twitter: Dani, Taylor, Todd, Sam, Beth, Brittany, Lynne, Lee, and so many more. Finally, thank you to all the dogs out there named Zeus. To be clear, I don't blame you.

Thank you to these publications, in which the following pieces, in one form or another, originally appeared:

Entropy, "Leda"

Small Poems, "For the Birds"

Cauldron Anthology, "I Can't Talk About It"

Feral, "Callisto," "The Effects of Lightning on the Human Body"

Little Death Lit, "His Worst-Case Scenario," "Her Worst-Case Scenario"

Anti-Heroin Chic, "Fettered," "Husk"

Southchild Lit, "In this Olympian House, We"

Orange Blossom Review, "How Many Hands Does a Trout Have?"

Anomaly, "How to Define Depression"

Detritus Online, "Metis"

Stentorian Bitch, "Michigan Tech University, Winter Festival 2006"

Door Is a Jar, "I Wish I Had the Foresight of Charlene Wood"

Kissing Dynamite, "When Depression Talks Over Me" (Pushcart Prize nominee)

Radical, "Danaë"

Lunch Ticket, "These Boots Are Made for Trauma" (2019 Twitter Poetry Contest Winner)

8 Poems, "When My Therapist Asks Me to Explain What 90 Seconds of Safety Feels Like, I Can Only Think of One Example"

About the Author

Lannie Stabile (she/her), a queer Detroiter, is the winner of OutWrite's 2020 Chapbook Competition in Poetry; the winning chapbook, "Strange Furniture," is out with Neon Hemlock Press. She is also a back-to-back finalist for the 2019/2020 and 2020/2021 Glass Chapbook Series and back-to-back semifinalist for the Button Poetry 2018 and 2019 Chapbook Contests. Lannie currently holds the position of Managing Editor at Barren Magazine and is a member of the MMPR Collective. She was named a 2020 Best of the Net finalist. Find her on Twitter @LannieStabile.

Made in the USA
Monee, IL
20 July 2021